Thomas Nelson Page

Polly - a Christmas Recollection

Thomas Nelson Page

Polly - a Christmas Recollection

ISBN/EAN: 9783337023546

Printed in Europe, USA, Canada, Australia, Japan

Cover: Foto ©Lupo / pixelio.de

More available books at **www.hansebooks.com**

POLLY

THOMAS·NELSON·PAGE

THE LIBRARY
OF
THE UNIVERSITY
OF CALIFORNIA
LOS ANGELES

To Aunt Mollie
   From Mabel
Christmas,
   Ninety Seven.

POLLY

IN UNIFORM STYLE

MARSE CHAN. A Tale of Old Virginia. Illustrated by W. T. Smedley.

MEH LADY. A Story of the War. Illustrated by C. S. Reinhart.

POLLY. A Christmas Recollection. Illustrated by A. Castaigne.

Each, small folio, $1.50.

"*The young man found it necessary to lean over and throw a steadying arm around her.*"

POLLY ✣ ✣ ✣ ✣ ✣
A CHRISTMAS RECOLLECTION
BY THOMAS NELSON PAGE
ILLUSTRATED BY A. CASTAIGNE

CHARLES SCRIBNER'S SONS
NEW YORK, 1894 ✣ ✣ ✣

Copyright, 1894, by
Charles Scribner's Sons

TROW DIRECTORY
PRINTING AND BOOKBINDING COMPANY
NEW YORK

LIST OF ILLUSTRATIONS

"*The young man found it necessary to lean over and throw a steadying arm around her.*"
Frontispiece.

Vignette heading. Page 1.

"*Drinkwater Torm fell sprawling on the floor.*"
Page 10.

"'*I will!*' *he said, throwing up his head.*" Page 22.

"*There he was standing on the bridge just before her.*" Page 30.

"*He made Torm, Charity, and a half-dozen younger house-servants dress him.*" Page 38.

IT was Christmas Eve. I remember it just as if it was yesterday. The Colonel had been pretending not to notice it, but when Drinkwater Torm* knocked over both the great candlesticks, and in his attempt to pick them up lurched over himself and fell sprawling on the floor, he yelled at him. Torm pulled himself together, and began an explanation, in which the point was that he had not "teched a drap in Gord knows how long," but the Colonel cut him short.

"Get out of the room, you drunken vagabond!" he roared.

Torm was deeply offended. He made a low, grand bow, and with as much dignity as his unsteady con-

* This spelling is used because he was called "Torm" until it became his name.

dition would admit, marched very statelily from the room, and passing out through the dining-room, where he stopped to abstract only one more drink from the long, heavy, cut-glass decanter on the sideboard, meandered to his house in the back-yard, where he proceeded to talk religion to Charity, his wife, as he always did when he was particularly drunk. He was expounding the vision of the golden candlestick, and the bowl and seven lamps and two olive-trees, when he fell asleep.

The roarer, as has been said, was the Colonel; the meanderer was Drinkwater Torm. The Colonel gave him the name, "because," he said, "if he were to drink water once he would die."

As Drinkwater closed the door, the Colonel continued, fiercely:

"Damme, Polly, I will! I'll sell him to-morrow morning; and if I can't sell him I'll give him away."

Polly, with troubled great dark eyes, was wheedling him vigorously.

"No: I tell you, I'll sell him.—'Misery in his back!' the mischief! he's a drunken, trifling, good-for-nothing nigger! and I have sworn to sell him a thousand—yes, ten thousand times; and now I'll have to do it to keep my word."

This was true. The Colonel swore this a dozen times a day—every time Torm got drunk, and as that had occurred very frequently for many years before Polly was born, he was not outside of the limit. Polly, however, was the only one this threat ever troubled. The Colonel knew he could no more have gotten on without Torm than his old open-faced watch, which looked for all the world like a model of himself, could have run without the mainspring. From tying his shoes and getting his shaving-water to making his juleps and lighting his candles, which was all he had to do, Drinkwater Torm was necessary to him. (I think he used to make the threat just to prove to himself that Torm did not own him; if so, he failed in his purpose —Torm did own him.) Torm knew it as well as he, or better; and while Charity, for private and wifely reasons, occasionally held the threat over him when his expoundings passed even her endurance, she knew it also.

Thus, Polly was the only one it deceived or frightened. It always deceived her, and she never rested until she had obtained Torm's reprieve "for just one more time." So on this occasion, before she got down from the Colonel's knees, she had given him in bargain "just one more squeeze," and received in return Torm's conditional pardon, "only till next time."

Everybody in the county knew the Colonel, and everybody knew Drinkwater Torm, and everybody who had been to the Colonel's for several years past (and that was nearly everybody in the county, for the Colonel kept open house) knew Polly. She had been placed in her chair by the Colonel's side at the club dinner on her first birthday after her arrival, and had been afterward placed on the table and allowed to crawl around among and in the dishes to entertain the gentlemen, which she did to the applause of every one, and of herself most of all; and from that time she had exercised in her kingdom the functions of both Vashti and Esther, and whatever Polly ordered was done. If the old inlaid piano in the parlor had been robbed of strings, it was all right, for Polly had taken them. Bob had cut them out for her, without a word of protest from anyone but Charity. The Colonel would have given her his heartstrings if Polly had required them.

She had owned him body and soul from the second he first laid eyes on her, when, on the instant he entered the room, she had stretched out her little chubby hands to him, and on his taking her had, after a few infantile caresses, curled up and, with her finger in her mouth, gone to sleep in his arms like a little white kitten.

Bob used to wonder in a vague, boyish way where the child got her beauty, for the Colonel weighed two hundred and fifty pounds, and was as ugly as a red head and thirty or forty years of Torm's mint-juleps piled on a somewhat reckless college career could make him; but one day, when the Colonel was away from home, Charity showed him a daguerreotype of a lady, which she got out of the top drawer of the Colonel's big secretary with the brass lions on it, and it looked exactly like Polly. It had the same great big dark eyes and the same soft white look, though Polly was stouter; for she was a great tomboy, and used to run wild over the place with Bob, climbing cherry-trees, fishing in the creek, and looking as blooming as a rose, with her hair all tangled over her pretty head, until she grew quite large, and the Colonel got her a tutor. He thought of sending her to a boarding-school, but the night he broached the subject he raised such a storm, and Polly was in such a tempest of tears, that he gave up the matter at once. It was well he did so, for Polly and Charity cried all night and Torm was so overcome that even next morning he could not bring the Colonel his shaving-water, and he had to shave with cold water for the first time in twenty years. He therefore employed a tutor. Most people said the child ought to have had a governess, and one or two single ladies of forgotten age in the neighborhood delicately hinted that they would gladly teach her; but the Colonel swore that he would have no women around him, and he would be eternally condemned if any should interfere with Polly: so he engaged Mr. Cranmer, and invited Bob to come over and go to school to him also, which he did; for his mother, who had up to that time taught him herself, was very poor, and was unable to send him to school, her husband, who was the Colonel's fourth cousin, having died largely indebted, and all of his property, except a small farm adjoining the Colonel's, and a few negroes, having gone into the General Court.

Bob had always been a great favorite with the Colonel, and ever since he was a small boy he had been used to coming over and staying with him.

He could gaff a chicken as well as Drinkwater Torm, which was a great accomplishment in the Colonel's eyes; for he had the best game-chickens in the county, and used to fight them, too, matching them against those of one or two of his neighbors who were similarly inclined, until Polly grew up and made him stop. He could tame a colt quicker than anybody on the plantation. Moreover he could shoot more partridges in a day than the Colonel, and could beat him shooting with a pistol as well, though the Colonel laid the fault of the former on his being so fat, and that of the latter on his spectacles. They used to practice with the Colonel's old pistols that hung in their holsters over the tester of his bed, and about which Drinkwater used to tell so many lies; for although they were kept loaded, and their brass-mounted butts peeping out of their leathern covers used to look ferocious enough to give some apparent ground for Torm's story of how "he and the Colonel had shot Judge Cabell spang through the heart," the Colonel always said that Cabell behaved very handsomely, and that the matter was arranged on the field without a shot. Even at that time some people said that Bob's mother was trying to catch the Colonel, and that if the Colonel did not look out she would yet be the mistress of his big plantation. And all agreed that the boy would come in for something handsome at the Colonel's death; for Bob was his cousin and his nearest male relative, if Polly *was* his niece, and he would hardly leave her all his property, especially as she was so much like her mother, with whom, as everybody knew, the Colonel had been desperately in love, but who had treated him badly, and, notwithstanding his big plantation and many negroes, had run away with his younger brother, and both of them had died in the South of yellow fever, leaving of all their children only this little Polly; and the Colonel had taken Drinkwater and Charity, and had travelled in his carriage all the way to Mississippi, to get and bring Polly back.

It was Christmas Eve when they reached home, and the Colonel had sent Drinkwater on a day ahead to have the fires made and the house aired for the baby; and when the carriage drove up that night you would have thought a queen was coming, sure enough.

Every hand on the plantation was up at the great house waiting for them, and every room in the house had a fire in it. (Torm had told the overseer so many lies that he had had the men cutting wood all day, although the regular supply was already cut.) And when Charity stepped out of the carriage, with the baby all bundled up in her arms, making a great show about keeping it wrapped up, and walked up the steps as slowly as if it were made of gold, you could have heard a pin drop; even the Colonel fell back, and spoke in a whisper. The great chamber was given up to the baby, the Colonel going to the wing room, where he always stayed after that. He spoke of sitting up all night to watch the child, but Charity assured him that she was not going to take her eyes off of her during the night, and with a promise to come in every hour and look after them, the Colonel went to his room, where he snored until nine o'clock the next morning.

But I was telling what people said about Bob's mother.

When the report reached the Colonel about the widow's designs, he took Polly on his knees and told her all about it, and then both laughed until the tears ran down the Colonel's face and dropped on his big flowered vest and on Polly's little blue frock; and he sent the widow next day a fine short-horned heifer to show his contempt of the gossip.

And now Bob was the better shot of the two; and they taught Polly to shoot also, and to load and unload the pistols, at which the Colonel was as proud as if one of his young stags had whipped an old rooster.

But they never could induce her to shoot at anything except a mark. She was the tenderest-hearted little thing in the world.

If her taste had been consulted she would have selected a crossbow, for it did not make such a noise, and she could shoot it without shutting her eyes; besides that, she could shoot it in the house, which, indeed, she did, until she had shot the eyes out of nearly all the bewigged gentlemen and bare-necked, long-fingered ladies on the walls. Once she came very near shooting Torm's eye out also; but this was an accident, though Drinkwater declared it was not, and tried to make out that Bob had put her up to it. "Dat's de mischievouses' boy Gord uver made," he said, complainingly, to Charity. Fortunately, his eye got well, and it gave him an excuse for staying half drunk for nearly a week; and afterward, like a dog that has once been lame in his hind-leg, whenever he saw Polly, and did not forget it, he squinted up that eye and tried to look miserable. Polly was quite a large girl then, and was carrying the keys (except when she lost them), though she could not have been more than twelve years old; for it was just after this that the birthday came when the Colonel gave her her first real silk dress. It was blue silk, and came from Richmond, and it was hard to tell which was the proudest, Polly, or Charity, or Drinkwater, or the Colonel. Torm got drunk before the dinner was over, "drinking de

"*Drinkwater Torm fell sprawling on the floor.*"

healthsh to de young mistis in de sky-blue robes what stands befo' de throne, you know," he explained to Charity, after the Colonel had ordered him from the dining-room, with promises of prompt sale on the morrow.

Bob was there, and it was the last time Polly ever sucked her thumb. She had almost gotten out of the habit anyhow, and it was in a moment of forgetfulness that she let Bob see her do it. He was a great tease, and when she was smaller had often worried her about it until she would fly at him and try to bite him with her little white teeth. On this occasion, however, she stood everything until he said that about a girl who wore a blue silk dress sucking her thumb; then she boxed his jaws. The fire flew from his eyes, but hers were even more sparkling. He paused for a minute, and then caught her in his arms and kissed her violently. She never sucked her thumb after that.

This happened out in front of her mammy's house, within which Torm was delivering a powerful exhortation on temperance; and, strange to say, Charity took Bob's side, while Torm espoused Polly's, and afterward said she ought to have "tooken a stick and knocked Marse Bob's head spang off." This, fortunately, Polly did not do (and when Bob went to the university afterward he was said to have the best head in his class). She just turned around and ran into the house, with her face very red. But she never slapped Bob after that. Not long after this he went off to college; for Mr. Cranmer, the tutor, said he already knew more than most college graduates did, and that it would be a shame for him not to have a university education. When the question of ways and means was mooted, the Colonel, who was always ready to lend money if he had it, and to borrow it if he did not, swore he would give him all the money he wanted; but, to his astonishment, Bob refused to accept it, and although the Colonel abused him for it, and asked Polly if she did not think he was a fool (which Polly did, for she was always ready to take and spend all the money he or any one else gave her), yet he did not like him the less for it, and he finally persuaded Bob to take it as a loan, and Bob gave him his bond.

The day before he left home he was over at the Colonel's, where they had a great dinner for him, and Polly presided in her newest silk dress (she had three then); and when Bob said good-by she slipped something into his hand, and ran away to her room, and when he looked at it, it was her ten-dollar gold piece, and he took it.

He was at college not quite three years, for his mother was taken sick, and he had to come home and nurse her; but he had stood first in most of his classes, and not lower than third in any; and he had thrashed the carpenter on Vinegar Hill, who was the bully of the town. So that although he did not take his degree, he had gotten the start which enabled him to complete his studies during the time he was taking care of his mother, which he did until her death, so that as soon as he was admitted to the bar he made his mark. It was his splendid defence of the man who shot the deputy-sheriff at the court-house on election day that brought him out as the Democratic candidate for the Constitutional Convention, where he made such a reputation as a speaker that the *Enquirer* declared him the rising man of the State; and even the *Whig* admitted that perhaps the Loco-foco party might find a leader to redeem it. Polly was just fifteen when she began to take an interest in politics; and although she read the papers diligently, especially the *Enquirer*, which her uncle never failed to abuse, yet she never could exactly satisfy herself which side was right; for the Colonel was a stanch Whig, while most people must have been Democrats, as Bob was elected by a big majority. She wanted to be on the Colonel's side, and made him explain everything to her, which he did to his own entire satisfaction, and to hers too, she tried to think; but when Bob came over to tea, which he very frequently did, and the Colonel and he got into a discussion, her uncle always seemed to her to get the worst of the argument; at any rate, he generally got very hot. This, however, might have been because Bob was so cool, while the Colonel was so hot-tempered.

Bob had grown up very handsome. His mouth was strong and firm, and his eyes were splendid. He was about six feet, and his shoulders were as broad as the Colonel's. She did not see him now as often as she did when he was a boy, but it was because he was kept so busy by his practice. (He used to get cases in three or four counties now, and big ones at that.) She knew, however, that she was just as good a friend of his as ever; indeed, she took the trouble to tell herself so. A compliment to him used to give her the greatest happiness, and would bring deeper roses into her cheeks. He was the greatest favorite with everybody. Torm thought that there was no one in the world like him. He had long ago forgiven him his many pranks, and said "he was the grettest gent'man in the county skusin him [Torm] and the Colonel."

and that "he al'ays handled heself to he raisin'," by which Torm made indirect reference to regular donations made to him by the aforesaid "gent'man," and particularly to an especially large benefaction then lately conferred. It happened one evening at the Colonel's, after dinner, when several guests, including Bob, were commenting on the perfections of various ladies who were visiting in the neighborhood that summer. The praises were, to Torm's mind, somewhat too liberally bestowed, and he had attempted to console himself by several visits to the pantry; but when all the list was disposed of, and Polly's name had not been mentioned, endurance could stand it no longer, and he suddenly broke in with his judgment that they "didn't none on 'em hol' a candle to his young mistis, whar wuz de ve'y pink an' flow'r on 'em all."

The Colonel, immensely pleased, ordered him out, with a promise of immediate sale on the morrow. But that evening, as he got on his horse, Bob slipped into his hand a five-dollar gold piece, and he told Polly that if the Colonel really intended to sell Torm, just to send him over to his house; he wanted the benefit of his judgment.

Polly, of course, did not understand his allusion, though the Colonel had told her of Torm's speech; but

Bob had a rose on his coat when he came out of the window, and the long pin in Polly's bodice was not fastened very securely, for it slipped, and she lost all her other roses, and he had to stoop and pick them up for her. Perhaps, though, Bob was simply referring to his having saved some money, for shortly afterward he came over one morning, and, to the Colonel's disgust, paid him down in full the amount of his bond. He attempted a somewhat formal speech of thanks, but broke down in it so lamentably that two juleps were ordered out by the Colonel to reinstate easy relations between them—an effect which apparently was not immediately produced—and the Colonel confided to Polly next day that since the fellow had been taken up so by those Loco-focos he was not altogether as he used to be.

"Why, he don't even drink his juleps clear," the old man asserted, as if he were charging him with, at the least, misprision of treason. "However," he added, softening as the excuse presented itself to his mind, "that may be because his mother was always so opposed to it. You know mint never would grow there," he pursued to Polly, who had heard him make the same observation, with the same astonishment, a hundred times. "Strangest thing I ever knew. But he's a confoundedly clever fellow, though, Polly," he continued, with a sudden reviving of the old-time affection. "Damme! I like him." And, as Polly's face turned a sweet carmine, added: "Oh, I forgot, Polly; didn't mean to swear; damme! if I did. It just slipped out. Now I haven't sworn before for a week; you know I haven't; yes, of course, I mean except *then*." For Polly, with softly fading color, was reading him the severest of lectures on his besetting sin, and citing an ebullition over Torm's failing of the day before. "Come and sit down on your uncle's knee and kiss him once as a token of forgiveness. Just one more squeeze," as the fair girlish arms were twined about his neck, and the sweetest of faces was pressed against his own rough cheek. "Polly, do you remember," asked the old man, holding her off from him and gazing at the girlish face fondly—"do you remember how, when you were a little scrap, you used to climb up on my knee and squeeze me, 'just once more,' to save that rascal Drinkwater, and how you used to say you were 'going to marry Bob' and me when you were grown up?"

Polly's memory, apparently, was not very good. That evening, however, it seemed much better, when, dressed all in soft white, and with cheeks reflecting the faint tints of the sunset clouds, she was strolling through the old flower-garden with a tall young fellow whose hat sat on his head with a jaunty air, and who was so very careful to hold aside the long branches of the rose-bushes. They had somehow gotten to recalling each in turn some incident of the old boy-and-girl days. Bob knew the main facts as well as she, but Polly remembered the little details and circumstances of each incident best, except those about the time they were playing "knucks" together. Then, singularly, Bob recollected most. He was positive that when she cried because he shot so hard, he had kissed her to make it well. Curiously, Polly's recollection failed again, and was only distinct about very modern matters. She remembered with remarkable suddenness that it was tea-time.

They were away down at the end of the garden, and her lapse of memory had a singular effect on Bob: for he turned quite pale, and insisted that she did remember it; and then said something about having wanted to see the Colonel, and having waited, and did so strangely that if that rose-bush had not caught her dress, he might have done something else. But the rose-bush caught her dress, and Polly, who looked really scared at it or at something, ran away just as the Colonel's voice was heard calling them to tea.

Bob was very silent at the table, and when he left, the Colonel was quite anxious about him. He asked Polly if she had not noticed his depression. Polly had not.

"That's just the way with you women," said the Colonel, testily. "A man might die under your very eyes, and you would not notice it. *I* noticed it, and I tell you the fellow's sick. I say he's sick!" he reiterated, with a little habit he had acquired since he had begun to grow slightly deaf. "I shall advise him to go away and have a little fling somewhere. He works too hard, sticks too close at home. He never goes anywhere except here, and he don't come here as he used to do. He ought to get married. Advise him to get married. Why don't he set up to Sally Brent or Malviny Pegram? He's a likely fellow, and they'd both take him—fools if they didn't:—I say they are fools if they didn't. What say?"

"I didn't say anything," said Polly, quietly going to the piano.

Her music often soothed the Colonel to sleep.

The next morning but one Bob rode over, and instead of hooking his horse to the fence as he usually did, he rode on around toward the stables. He greeted Torm, who was in the backyard, and after extracting some preliminary observations from him respecting the "misery in his back," he elicited the further facts that Miss Polly was going down the road to dine at the Pegrams', of which he had some intimation before, and that the Colonel was down on the river farm, but would be back about two o'clock. He rode on.

At two o'clock promptly Bob returned. The Colonel had not yet gotten home. He, however, dismounted, and, tying his horse, went in. He must have been tired of sitting down, for he now walked up and down the portico without once taking a seat.

"Marse Bob 'll walk heself to death," observed Charity to Torm, from her door.

Presently the Colonel came in, bluff, warm, and hearty. He ordered dinner from the front gate as he dismounted, and juleps from the middle of the walk, greeted Bob with a cheeriness which that gentleman in vain tried to imitate, and was plumped down in his great split-bottomed chair, wiping his red head with his still redder bandana handkerchief, and abusing the weather, the crops, the newspapers, and his overseer before Bob could get breath to make a single remark. When he did, he pitched in on the weather.

That is a safe topic at all times. It was astonishing how much comfort Bob got out of it this afternoon. He talked about it until dinner began to come in across the yard, the blue china dishes gleaming in the hands of Phœbe and her numerous corps of ebon and mahogany assistants, and Torm brought out the juleps, with the mint looking as if it were growing in the great silver cans, with frosted work all over the sides.

Dinner was rather a failure, so far as Bob was concerned. Perhaps he missed something that usually graced the table; perhaps only his body was there, while he himself was down at Miss Malviny Pegram's; perhaps he had gone back and was unfastening an impertinent rose-bush from a filmy white dress in the summer twilight; perhaps—; but anyhow he was so silent and abstracted that the Colonel rallied him good-humoredly, which did not help matters.

They had adjourned to the porch, and had been there for some time, when Bob broached the subject of his visit.

"Colonel," he said, suddenly, and wholly irrelevant to everything that had gone before, "there is a matter I want to speak to you about—a—ah—we—a little matter of great importance to—ah—myself." He was getting very red and confused, and the Colonel instantly divining the matter, and secretly flattering himself, and determining to crow over Polly, said, to help him out:

"Aha, you rogue, I knew it. Come up to the scratch, sir. So you are caught at last. Ah, you sly fox! It's the very thing you ought to do. Why, I know half a dozen girls who'd jump at you. I knew it. I said so the other night. Polly—"

Bob was utterly off his feet by this time. "I want to ask your consent to marry Polly," he blurted out desperately: "I love her."

"The devil you do!" exclaimed the Colonel. He could say no more; he simply sat still, in speechless, helpless, blank amazement. To him Polly was still a little girl climbing his knees, and an emperor might not aspire to her.

"Yes, sir, I do," said Bob, calm enough now—growing cool as the Colonel became excited. "I love her, and I want her."

"Well, sir, you can't have her!" roared the Colonel, pulling himself up from his seat in the violence of his refusal. He looked like a tawny lion whose lair had been invaded.

Bob's face paled, and a look came on it that the Colonel recalled afterward, and which he did not re-

"'I will!' he said, throwing up his head."

member ever to have seen on it before, except once, when, years ago, some one shot one of his dogs—a look made up of anger and of dogged resolution. "I will!" he said, throwing up his head and looking the Colonel straight in the eyes, his voice perfectly calm, but his eyes blazing, the mouth drawn close, and the lines of his face as if they had been carved in granite.

"I'll be —— if you shall!" stormed the Colonel: "the King of England should not have her!" and, turning, he stamped into the house and slammed the door behind him.

Bob walked slowly down the steps and around to the stables, where he ordered his horse. He rode home across the fields without a word, except, as he jumped his horse over the line fence, "I will have her," he repeated, between his fast-set teeth.

That evening Polly came home all unsuspecting anything of the kind; the Colonel waited until she had taken off her things and come down in her fresh muslin dress. She surpassed in loveliness the rose-buds that lay on her bosom, and the impertinence that could dare aspire to her broke over the old man in a fresh wave. He had nursed his wrath all the evening.

"Polly!" he blurted out, suddenly rising with a jerk from his arm-chair, and unconsciously striking an attitude before the astonished girl, "do you want to marry Bob?"

"Why, no," cried Polly, utterly shaken out of her composure by the suddenness and vehemence of the attack.

"I *knew it!*" declared the Colonel, triumphantly. "It was a piece of cursed impertinence!" and he worked himself up to such a pitch of fury, and grew so red in the face, that poor Polly, who had to steer between two dangers, was compelled to employ all her arts to soothe the old man and keep him out of a fit of apoplexy. She learned the truth, however, and she learned something which, until that time, she had never known; and though, as she kissed her uncle "good-night," she made no answer to his final shot of, "Well, I'm glad we are not going to have any nonsense about the fellow; I have made up my mind, and we'll treat his impudence as it deserves," she locked her door carefully when she was within her own room, and the next morning she said she had a headache.

Bob did not come that day.

If the Colonel had not been so hot-headed—that is, if he had not been a man—things would doubtless have straightened themselves out in some of those mysterious ways in which the hardest knots into which two young peoples' affairs contrive to get untangle themselves; but being a man, he must needs, man-like, undertake to manage according to his own plan, which is always the wrong one.

When, therefore, he announced to Polly at the breakfast-table that morning that she would have no further annoyance from that fellow's impertinence; for he had written him a note apologizing for leaving him abruptly in his own house the day before, but forbidding him, in both their names, to continue his addresses, or, indeed, to put his foot on the place again; he fully expected to see Polly's face brighten, and to receive her approbation and thanks. What, then, was his disappointment to see her face grow distinctly white. All she said was, "Oh, uncle!"

It was unfortunate that the day was Sunday, and that the Colonel went with her to church (which she insisted on attending, notwithstanding her headache), and was by when she met Bob. They came on each other suddenly. Bob took off his hat and stood like a soldier on review, erect, expectant, and a little pale. The Colonel, who had almost forgotten his "impertinence," and was about to shake hands with him as usual, suddenly remembered it, and drawing himself up, stepped to the other side of Polly, and handed her by the younger gentleman as if he were protecting her from a mob. Polly, who had been looking anxiously everywhere but in the right place, meaning to give Bob a smile which would set things straight, caught his eye only at that second, and felt rather than saw the change in his attitude and manner. She tried to throw him the smile, but it died in her eyes, and even after her back was turned she was sensible of his defiance. She went into church, and dropped down on her knees in the far end of her pew, with her little heart needing all the consolations of her religion.

The man she prayed hardest for did not come into church that day.

Things went very badly after that, and the knots got tighter and tighter. An attempt which Bob made to loosen them failed disastrously, and the Colonel, who was the best-hearted man in the world, but whose prejudices were made of wrought iron, took it into his head that Bob had insulted him, and Polly's indirect efforts at pacification aroused him to such an extent that for the first time in his life he was almost hard with her. He conceived the absurd idea that she was sacrificing herself for Bob on account of her friendship for him, and that it was his duty to protect her against herself, which, man-like, he proceeded to do in his own fashion, to poor Polly's great distress.

She was devoted to her uncle, and knew the strength of his affection for her. On the other hand, Bob and she had been friends so long. She never could remember the time when she did not have Bob. But he had never said a word of love to her in his life. To be sure, on that evening in the garden she had known it just as well as if he had fallen on his knees at her feet. She knew his silence was just because he had owed her uncle the money; and oh! if she just hadn't gotten frightened; and oh! if her uncle just hadn't done it; and oh! she was so unhappy! The poor little thing, in her own dainty, white-curtained room, where were the books and things he had given her, and the letters he had written her, used to—but that is a secret. Anyhow, it was not because he was gone. She knew that was not the reason—indeed, she very often said so to herself; it was because he had been treated so unjustly, and suffered so, and she had done it all. And she used to introduce many new petitions into her prayers, in which, if there was not any name expressed, she felt that it would be understood, and the blessings would reach him just the same.

The summer had gone, and the Indian summer had

come in its place, hazy, dreamy, and sad. It always made Polly melancholy, and this year, although the weather was perfect, she was affected, she said, by the heat, and did not go out of doors much. So presently her cheeks were not as blooming as they had been, and even her great dark eyes lost some of their lustre; at least, Charity thought so, and said so too, not only to Polly, but to her master, whom she scared half to death; and who, notwithstanding that Dr. Stopper was coming over every other day to see a patient on the plantation, and that the next day was the time for his regular visit, put a boy on a horse that night and sent him with a note urging him to come the next morning to breakfast.

The doctor came, and spent the day: examined Polly's lungs and heart, prescribed out-door exercise, and left something less than a bushel-basketful of medicines for her to take.

Polly was, at the time of his visit, in a very excited state, for the Colonel had, with a view of soothing her, the night before delivered a violent philippic against marriage in general, and in particular against marriage with "impudent young puppies who did not know their places;" and he had proposed an extensive tour, embracing all the United States and Canada, and intended to cover the entire winter and spring following. Polly, who had stood as much as she could stand, finally rebelled, and had with flashing eyes and mantling cheeks espoused Bob's cause with a courage and dash which had almost routed the old Colonel. "Not that he was anything to her except a friend," she was most careful to explain; but she was tired of hearing her "friend" assailed, and she thought that it was the highest compliment a man could pay a woman, etc., etc., for all of which she did a great deal of blushing in her own room afterwards.

Thus it happened, that she was both excited and penitent the next day, and thinking to make some atonement, and at the same time to take the prescribed exercise, which would excuse her from taking the medicines, she filled a little basket with goodies to take old Aunt Betty at the Far Quarters; and thus it happened, that, as she was coming back along the path which ran down the meadow on the other side of the creek which was the dividing line between the two plantations, and was almost at the foot-bridge that Somebody had made for her so carefully with logs cut out of his own woods, and the long shadows of the willows made it gloomy, and everything was so still that she had grown very lonely and unhappy—thus it happened, that just as she was thinking how kind he had been about making the bridge and hand-rail so strong, and about everything, and how cruel he must think her, and how she would never see him any more as she used to do, she turned the clump of willows to step up on the log, and there he was standing on the bridge just before her, looking down into her eyes! She tried to get by him—she remembered that afterwards; but he was so mean. It was always a little confused in her memory, and she could never recall exactly how it was. She was sure, however, that it was because he was so pale that she said it, and that she did not begin to cry until afterwards, and that it was because he would not listen to her explanation; and that she didn't let him do it, she could not help it, and she did not know her head was on his shoulder.

Anyhow, when she got home that evening her improvement was so apparent that the Colonel called Charity in to note it, and declared that Virginia country doctors were the finest in the world, and that Stopper was the greatest doctor in the State. The change was wonderful, indeed; and the old gilt mirror, with its gauze-covered frame, would never have known for the sad-eyed Polly of the day before the bright,

"*There he was standing on the bridge just before her.*"

happy maiden that stood before it now and smiled at the beaming face which dimpled at its own content.

Old Betty's was a protracted pleurisy, and the good things Polly carried her daily did not tend to shorten the sickness. Ever afterwards she "blessed the Lord for dat chile" whenever Polly's name was mentioned. She would doubtless have included Bob in her benison had she known how sympathetic he was during this period.

But although he was inspecting that bridge every afternoon regularly, notwithstanding Polly's oft-reiterated wish and express orders as regularly declared, no one knew a word of all this. And it was a bow drawn at a venture when, on the evening that Polly had tried to carry out her engagement to bring her uncle around, the old man had said, "Why, hoity-toity! the young rascal's cause seems to be thriving." She had been so confident of her success that she was not prepared for failure, and it struck her like a fresh blow; and though she did not cry until she got into her own room, when she got there she threw herself on the bed and cried herself to sleep. "It was so cruel in him," she said to herself, "to desire me never to speak to him again! And, oh! if he should really catch him on the place and shoot him!" The pronouns in our language were probably invented by young women.

The headache Polly had the next morning was not invented. Poor little thing! her last hope was gone. She determined to bid Bob good-by, and never see him again. She had made up her mind to this on her knees, so she knew she was right. The pain it cost her satisfied her that she was.

She was firmly resolved when she set out that afternoon to see old Betty, who was in everybody's judgment except her own quite convalescent, and whom Dr. Stopper pronounced entirely well. She wavered a little in her resolution when, descending the path along the willows, which were leafless now, she caught sight of a tall figure loitering easily up the meadow, and she abandoned—that is, she forgot it altogether when, having doubtfully suggested it, she was suddenly enfolded in a pair of strong arms, and two gray eyes, lighting a handsome face strong with the self-confidence which women love, looked down into hers.

Then he proposed it!

Her heart almost stood still at his boldness. But he was so strong, so firm, so reasonable, so self-reliant, and yet so gentle, she could not but listen to him. Still she refused—and she never did consent; she forbade him ever to think of it again. Then she begged him never to come there again, and told him of her uncle's threats, and of her fears for him; and then, when he laughed at them, she begged him never, never, under any circumstances, to take any notice of what her uncle might do or say, but rather to stand still and be shot dead; and then, when Bob promised this, she burst into tears, and he had to hold her and comfort her like a little girl.

It was pretty bad after that, and but for Polly's outdoor exercise she would undoubtedly have succumbed. It seemed as if something had come between her and her uncle. She no longer went about singing like a bird. She suffered under the sense of being misunderstood, and it was so lonely! He too was oppressed by it. Even Torm shared in it, and his expositions assumed a cast terrific in the last degree.

It was now December.

One evening it culminated. The weather had been too bad for Polly to go out, and she was sick. Finally Stopper was sent for. Polly, who, to use Charity's expression, was "pestered till she was fractious," rebelled flatly, and refused to keep her bed or to take the medicines prescribed. Charity backed her. Torm got drunk. The Colonel was in a fume, and declared his intention to sell Torm next morning, as usual, and to take Charity and Polly and go to Europe. This was well enough; but to Polly's consternation, when she came to breakfast next morning, she found that the old man's plans had ripened into a scheme to set out on the very next day for Louisiana and New Orleans, where he proposed to spend the winter looking after some plantations she had, and showing her something of the world. Polly remonstrated, rebelled, cajoled. It was all in vain. Stopper had seriously frightened the old man about her health, and he was adamant. Preparations were set on foot; the brown hair trunks, with their lines of staring brass tacks, were raked out and dusted; the Colonel got into a fever, ordered up all the negroes in the yard, and gave instructions from the front door, like a major-general reviewing his troops; got Torm, Charity, and all the others into a wild flutter; attempted to superintend Polly's matters; made her promises of fabulous gifts; became reminiscent, and told marvelous stories of his old days, which Torm corroborated; and so excited Polly and the plantation generally, that from old Betty, who came from the Far Quarters for the purpose of taking it in, down to the blackest little dot on the place, there was not one who did not get into a wild whirl, and talk as if they were all going to New Orleans the next morning, with Joe Rattler on the boot.

Polly had, after a stout resistance, surrendered to her fate, and packed her modest trunk with very mingled feelings. Under other circumstances she would have enjoyed the trip immensely; but she felt now as if it were parting from Bob forever. Her heart was in her throat all day, and even the excitement of packing could not drive away the feeling. She knew she would never see him again. She tried to work out what the end would be. Would he die, or would he marry Malviny Pegram? Every one said she would just suit him, and she'd certainly marry him if he asked her.

The sun was shining over the western woods. Bob rode down that way in the afternoon, even when it was raining; he had told her so. He would think it cruel of her to go away thus, and never even let him know. She would at least go and tell him good-by. So she did.

Bob's face paled suddenly when she told him all, and that look which she had not seen often before settled on it. Then he took her hand and began to explain everything to her. He told her that he had loved her all her life; showed her how she had inspired him to work for and win every success that he had achieved; how it had been her work even more than his. Then he laid before her the life plans he had formed, and proved how they were all for her, and for her only. He made it all so clear, and his voice was so confident, and his face so earnest, as he pleaded and proved it step by step, that she felt, as she leaned against him and he clasped her closely, that he was right, and that she could not part from him.

That evening Polly was unusually silent; but the Colonel thought she had never been so sweet. She petted him until he swore that no man on earth was worthy of her, and that none should ever have her.

After tea she went to his room to look over his clothes (her especial work), and would let no one, not even her mammy, help her; and when the Colonel insisted on coming in to tell her some more concerning the glories of New Orleans in his day, she finally put him out and locked the door on him.

She was very strange all the evening. As they were to start the next morning, the Colonel was for retiring early; but Polly would not go; she loitered around, hung about the old fellow, petted him, sat on his knee and kissed him, until he was forced to insist on her going to bed. Then she said good-night, and astonished the Colonel by throwing herself into his arms and bursting out crying.

The old man soothed her with caresses and baby talk, such as he used to comfort her with when she was a little girl, and when she became calm he handed her to her door as if she had been a duchess.

The house was soon quiet, except that once the Colonel heard Polly walking in her room, and mentally determined to chide her for sitting up so late. He, however, drifted off from the subject when he heard some of his young mules galloping around the yard, and he made a sleepy resolve to sell them all, or to dismiss his overseer next day for letting them out of the lot. Before he had quite determined which he should do, he dropped off to sleep again.

It was possibly about this time that a young man lifted into her saddle a dark-habited little figure, whose face shone very white in the starlight, and whose tremulous voice would have suggested a refusal had it not been drowned in the deep, earnest tone of her lover. Although she declared that she could not think of doing it, she had on her hat and furs and riding-habit when Bob came. She did, indeed, really beg him to go away; but a few minutes later a pair of horses cantered down the avenue toward the lawn gate, which shut with a bang that so frightened the little lady on the bay mare that the young man found it necessary to lean over and throw a steadying arm around her.

For the first time in her life Polly saw the sun rise in North Carolina, and a few hours later a gentle-voiced young clergyman, whose sweet-faced wife was wholly carried away by Polly's beauty, received under protest Bob's only gold piece, a coin which he twisted from his watch-chain with the promise to quadruple it if he would preserve it until he could redeem it.

When Charity told the Colonel next morning that Polly was gone, the old man for the first time in fifty years turned perfectly white. Then he fell into a consuming rage, and swore until Charity would not have been much surprised to see the devil appear in visible shape and claim him on the spot. He cursed Bob, cursed himself, cursed Torm, Charity, and the entire female sex individually and collectively, and then, seized by a new idea, he ordered his horse, that he might pursue the runaways, threatened an immediate sale of his whole plantation, and the instantaneous death of Bob, and did in fact get down his great brass-mounted pistols, and lay them by him as he made Torm, Charity, and a half-dozen younger house-servants dress him.

"He made Torm, Charity, and a half-dozen younger house-servants dress him."

Dressing and shaving occupied him about an hour —he always averred that a gentleman could not dress like a gentleman in less time—and, still breathing out threatenings and slaughter, he marched out of his room, making Torm and Charity follow him, each with a pistol. Something prompted him to stop and inspect them in the hall. Taking first one and then the other, he examined them curiously.

"Well, I'll be ——!" he said, dryly, and flung both of them crashing through the window. Turning, he ordered waffles and hoe-cakes for breakfast, and called for the books to have prayers.

Polly had utilized the knowledge she had gained as a girl, and had unloaded both pistols the night before, and rammed the balls down again without powder, so as to render them harmless.

By breakfast time Torm was in a state of such advanced intoxication that he was unable to walk through the back yard gate, and the Colonel was forced to content himself with sending by Charity a message that he would get rid of him early the next morning. He straitly enjoined Charity to tell him, and she as solemnly promised to do so. "Yes, suh, *I* gwi' tell him," she replied, with a faint tone of being wounded at his distrust; and she did.

She needed an outlet.

Things got worse. The Colonel called up the overseer and gave new orders, as if he proposed to change everything. He forbade any mention of Polly's name, and vowed that he would send for Mr. Steep, his lawyer, and change his will to spite all creation. This humor, instead of wearing off, seemed to grow worse as the time stretched on, and Torm actually grew sober in the shadow that had fallen on the plantation. The Colonel had Polly's room nailed up and shut himself up in the house.

The negroes discussed the condition of affairs in awed undertones, and watched him furtively whenever he passed. Various opinions by turns prevailed. Aunt Betty, who was regarded with veneration, owing partly to the interest the lost Polly had taken in her illness, and partly to her great age (to which she annually added three years) prophesied that he was going to die "in torments," just like some old uncle of his whom no one else had ever heard of until now, but who was raked up by her to serve as a special example. The chief resemblance seemed to be a certain "rankness in cussin'."

Things were certainly going badly, and day by day they grew worse. The Colonel became more and more morose.

"He don' even quoil no mo'," Torm complained pathetically to Charity. "He jes set still and study. I 'feard he gwine 'stracted."

It was, indeed, lamentable. It was accepted on the plantation that Miss Polly had gone for good—some said down to Louisiana—and would never come back any more. The prevailing impression was that, if she did, the Colonel would certainly kill Bob. Torm had not a doubt of it.

Thus matters stood three days before Christmas. The whole plantation was plunged in gloom. It would be the first time since Miss Polly was a baby that they had not had "a big Christmas."

Torm's lugubrious countenance one morning seemed to shock the Colonel out of his lethargy. He asked how many days there would be before Christmas, and learning that there were but three, he ordered preparations to be made for a great feast and a big time generally. He had the wood-pile replenished as usual, got up his presents, and superintended the Christmas operations himself, as Polly used to do. But it was sad work, and when Torm and Charity retired Christmas Eve night, although Torm had imbibed plentifully, and the tables were all spread for the great dinner for the servants next day, there was no peace in

Torm's discourse; it was all of wrath and judgment to come.

He had just gone to sleep when there was a knock at the door.

"Who dat out dyah?" called Charity. "You niggers better go 'long to bed."

The knock was repeated.

"Who dat out dyah, I say?" queried Charity, testily. "Whyn't you go 'long 'way from dat do'? Torm, Torm, dee's somebody at de do'," she said, as the knocking was renewed.

Torm was hard to wake, but at length he got up and moved slowly to the door, grumbling to himself all the time.

When finally he undid the latch, Charity, who was in bed, heard him exclaim, "Well, name o' Gord! good Gord A'mighty!" and burst into a wild explosion of laughter.

In a second she too was outside of the door, and had Polly in her arms, laughing, jumping, hugging, and kissing her while Torm executed a series of caracoles around them.

"Whar Marse Bob?" asked both negroes, finally, in a breath.

"Hello, Torm! How are you, Mam' Charity?"

called that gentleman, cheerily, coming up from where he had been fastening the horses; and Charity, suddenly mindful of her peculiar appearance and of the frosty air, "scuttled" into the house, conveying her young mistress with her.

Presently she came out dressed, and invited Bob in too. She insisted on giving them something to eat; but they had been to supper, and Polly was much too excited hearing about her uncle to eat anything. She cried a little at Charity's description of him, which she tried to keep Bob from seeing, but he saw it, and had to—however, when they got ready to go home, Polly insisted on going to the yard and up on the porch, and when there, she actually kissed the window-blind of the room whence issued a muffled snore suggestive at least of some degree of forgetfulness. She wanted Bob to kiss it too, but that gentleman apparently found something else more to his taste, and her entreaty was drowned in another sound.

Before they remounted their horses Polly carried Bob to the greenhouse, where she groped around in the darkness for something, to Bob's complete mystification. "Doesn't it smell sweet in here?" she asked.

"I don't smell anything but that mint bed you've been walking on," he laughed.

As they rode off, leaving Torm and Charity standing in the road, the last thing Polly said was, "Now be sure you tell him—nine o'clock."

"Umm! I know he gwi' sell me den sho 'nough," said Torm, in a tone of conviction, as the horses cantered away in the frosty night.

Once or twice, as they galloped along, Bob made some allusion to the mint bed on which Polly had stepped, to which she made no reply. But as he helped her down at her own door, he asked, "What in the world have you got there?"

"Mint," said she, with a little low, pleased laugh.

By light next morning it was known all over the plantation that Miss Polly had returned. The rejoicing, however, was clouded by the fear that nothing would come of it.

In Charity's house it was decided that Torm should break the news. Torm was doubtful on the point as the time drew near, but Charity's mind never wavered. Finally he went in with his master's shaving-water, having first tried to establish his courage by sundry pulls at a black bottle. He essayed three times to deliver the message, but each time his courage failed, and he hastened out under pretence of the water having gotten cold. The last time he attracted Charity's attention.

"Name o' Gord, Torm, you gwine to scawl hawgs?" she asked, sarcastically.

The next time he entered the Colonel was in a fume of impatience, so he had to fix the water. He set down the can, and bustled about with hypocritical industry. The Colonel, at last, was almost through; Torm retreated to the door. As his master finished, he put his hand on the knob, and turning it, said, "Miss Polly come home larse night; sh' say she breakfast at nine o'clock."

Slapbang! came the shaving-can, smashing against the door, just as he dodged out, and the roar of the Colonel followed him across the hall.

When finally their master appeared on the portico, Torm and Charity were watching in some doubt whether he would not carry out on the spot his long-threatened purpose. He strode up and down the long porch, evidently in great excitement.

"He's turrible dis mornin'," said Torm; "he th'owed de whole kittle o' b'ilin' water at me."

"Pity he didn' scawl you to death," said his wife, sympathizingly. She thought Torm's awkwardness had destroyed Polly's last chance. Torm resorted to his black bottle, and proceeded to talk about the lake of brimstone and fire.

Up and down the portico strode the old Colonel. His horse was at the rack, where he was always brought before breakfast. (For twenty years he had probably never missed a morning.) Finally he walked down, and looked at the saddle; of course, it was all wrong. He fixed it, and, mounting, rode off in the opposite direction to that whence his invitation had come. Charity, looking out of her door, inserted into her diatribe against "all wuthless, drunken, fool niggers" a pathetic parenthesis to the effect that "Ef Marster meet Marse Bob dis mornin', de don' be a hide nor hyah left o'nyah one on 'em; an' dat lamb over dyah maybe got oystehers waitin' for him too."

Torm was so much impressed that he left Charity and went out of doors.

The Colonel rode down the plantation, his great gray horse quivering with life in the bright winter sunlight. He gave him the rein, and he turned down a cross-road which led out of the plantation into the main highway. Mechanically he opened the gate and rode out. Before he knew where he was he was through the wood, and his horse had stopped at the next gate. It was the gate of Bob's place. The house stood out bright and plain among the yard trees: lines of blue smoke curled up almost straight from the chimneys;

and he could see two or three negroes running backward and forward between the kitchen and the house. The sunlight glistened on something in the hand of one of them, and sent a ray of dazzling light all the way to the old man. He knew it was a plate or a dish. He took out his watch and glanced at it; it was five minutes to nine o'clock. He started to turn around to go home. As he did so, the memory of all the past swept over him, and of the wrong that had been done him. He would go in and show them his contempt for them by riding in and straight out again; and he actually unlatched the gate and went in. As he rode across the field he recalled all that Polly had been to him from the time when she had first stretched out her arms to him; all the little ways by which she had brought back his youth, and had made his house home, and his heart soft again. Every scene came before him as if to mock him. He felt once more the touch of her little hand; heard again the sound of her voice as it used to ring through the old house and about the grounds; saw her and Bob as children romping about his feet, and he gave a great gulp as he thought how desolate the house was now. He sat up in his saddle stiffer than ever. D—— him! he would enter his very house, and there to his face and hers denounce him for his baseness; he pushed his horse to a trot. Up to the yard gate he rode, and, dismounting, hitched his horse to the fence, and slamming the gate fiercely behind him, stalked up the walk with his heavy whip clutched fast in his hand. Up the walk and up the steps, without a pause, his face set as grim as rock, and purple with suppressed emotion; for a deluge of memories was overwhelming him.

The door was shut; they had locked it on him; but he would burst it in, and—Ah! what was that?

The door flew suddenly open; there was a cry, a spring, a vision of something swam before his eyes, and two arms were clasped about his neck, while he was being smothered with kisses from the sweetest mouth in the world, and a face made up of light and laughter, yet tearful, too, like a dew-bathed flower, was pressed to his, and before the Colonel knew it he had, amid laughter and sobs and caresses, been borne into the house, and pressed down at the daintiest little breakfast-table eyes ever saw, set for three persons, and loaded with steaming dishes, and with a great fresh julep by the side of his plate, and Tom standing behind his chair, whilst Bob was helping him to "oystchers," and Polly, with dimpling face, was attempting the exploit of pouring out his coffee without moving her arm from around his neck.

The first thing he said after he recovered his breath was, "Where did you get this mint?"

Polly broke into a peal of rippling, delicious laughter, and tightened the arm about his neck.

"Just one more squeeze," said the Colonel; and as she gave it he said, with the light of it all breaking on him, "Damme if I don't sell you! or, if I can't sell you, I'll give you away—that is, if he'll come over and live with us."

That evening, after the great dinner, at which Polly had sat in her old place at the head of the table, and Bob at the foot, because the Colonel insisted on sitting where Polly could give him one more squeeze, the whole plantation was ablaze with "Christmas," and Drinkwater Torm, steadying himself against the sideboard, delivered a discourse on peace on earth and good-will to men so powerful and so eloquent that the Colonel, delighted, rose and drank his health, and said, "Damme if I ever sell him again!"

www.ingramcontent.com/pod-product-compliance
Lightning Source LLC
Chambersburg PA
CBHW020731100426
42735CB00038B/1872